POEMS BY FRANCIS MARSHALL

This book is sold subject to the condition that it shall not, by way of trade or otherwise, be lent, re-sold, hired out, photocopied or held in any retrieval system, or otherwise circulated without the publishers prior consent in any form of binding or cover other than that in which this is published and without a similar condition including this condition being imposed on the subsequent purchaser.

Printed and bound in the U.K.

Avon Books
London
First published 1993
© Francis Marshall 1993
ISBN 1 897960 45 X

Poems

by

Francis Marshall

AVON BOOKS
AUBREY HOUSE, 83/85, BRIDGE ROAD
EAST MOLESEY, SURREY KT8 9HH

NATURE

Winter to Springtime

Delicate line between Winter and Spring,
Such coldness, fluctuating body warmth,
Same clothes of winter cover shuffling forms
Treading weary paths with solid footwear.
Are there no signs separating these seasons?

Bare trees parade the same
Only to glimpse early blooms of flowers,
Cold winter blow!
Sure it is winter not spring!
Heavy clouds, light clouds, rain, hazy sunshine,
Light winds, strong winds, gusts, even snow
All identify wintery weather?
No, the seasonal I pray to call
Showing activities of man:

Farmer labouring on the land;
Chip arrows, disc carriers, rollers
And tractors break winter's ground - darkening soil.
Seed drill rows plant the tiny embryos:
Gardens and parks battle with the artillery
Of landscaping beauty.
Discern I try, but cannot, the delicate line between.

Arid Plants and Flowers

Fragrance fills the flower patch,
Scents spring from scarlet blooms,
Each flower pouring forth beauty.
Dry spells inhibit growth,
The tap-root boring down deeper;
Natural living water at a premium,
Authority restrict abundant flow,
Human help urgently called,
Carry liquid life to the thirsty.
Lift up heads again, drooping stems
Tap water revives, Will to straighten.
Evening here, some coolness:
Tomorrow again, sun and heat.
Hot dry summer in chalky bed
Roots, stems, leaves, petals
Dry, dry, dry no relief,
Scarce drops of rain tantalize.
When will the down-pour come?
Frustrated flowers and plants droop
In the day of the scorching sun,
The red hot summer never gives up
Man evening after evening waters trough,
Survival of the fittest, order of the day.
Don't weaken, roses, rhododendrons and others
Look above, sky with small clouds;
Wind blow the rain this way?
Morning fresh with breeze:
Black heavens lining the sky,
Eureka! sense the change.

Rain coming in from the sea,
Fresh quenching natural water,
To make the roots live again.

Wind So Cold

Wind, wind, wind buffeting the sea
Summer fades to retreat and hibernate;
The turbulent Autumn blows cold.
Whistling winds singing high notes:
Rain blustering, cascading angry bursts
Darkness penetrates the cold night:
The cold night penetrates the darkness.
Bitter, fierce attacking tempest
Zephyr rising, rising to crescendo,
Battering and bruising all that is frail.
Bent double under the strain
Humans struggle against force,
Loving tempestuous blizzard,
Show mercy, ease angryness
Mistral cold to simoom wind.
The sun smiles through,
But only weak like an invalid,
Soon inclement weather numbs
Advancing into Winter gelidity.

Petals So Blue

Wandering, wandering through the park
Aimlessly, slowly walking,
Not heeding.
Unconscious of reality there,
Behold, exquisite blue petals,
Areas and areas of blueness
Sparkling and directing blue rays
From a bright sun.
Am I dreaming?
No, meandering.

Multitudes of spring blossoms
Shine brilliant rays in all directions:
Petals flowing like waves in a breeze.
Park, have you come to life,
From uniform stillness
To overflowing blushness of blue,
Mirroring the blue freshness
Of a damsel?

Perpetual movement, swaying
In each other's arms
Like courting couples:
Peaceful and serene
Making the most of your
Short-lived stay.

Heavy Seas

Walking along the cliffs -
It's been June now July -
Is the weather going to change,
To ease the pain of the waves?
With white foam they lash the shore,
The wind must drop, the sun shine;
The waves are mountain high
No different from the Winter's storm.
Has our Summer caught a cold?
To make it sneeze and buffet the earth.
The fishermen must now stay ashore
Until the seas calm down their fury;
Black clouds deepen the gloom,
Cold winds fresh from the swell.
The heavy seas will not abate:
Come, let's have an Indian summer
And calm the fury that rocks the sea,
But, alas, oh this tempest!

Dying Plants

Deeply pre-occupied in my room,
Not knowing what there is to do;
Sitting down to read a book
Or absent-mindedly thinking.
Sometimes studying literature
Forgetting a life is dying:
After much time has passed
My eye wander over the furniture
Observing a browny haze.
Alas, the leaves of the plants are turning brown;
Are they dying or are they dead?
Jumping up onto the bed
I take the pots down and look within;
Not one drop of moisture can I see.
The neglected plants are bone dry,
I hope and pray they will not die.
Quickly under the tap they go
Hoping to revive them soon,
and bring back their green hue.

The Cold Backend

Bleak days approaching fast
The cold weather has come at last.
Inside warm and cosified
In our hamlets we abide.
Stark wintry winds blow!
Sitting in front of fires that glow;
Outside cascading tempest
Fiercely gusting, no rest.
Rain squalls drenching all,
Water flowing down like a waterfall.
Dark nights expose winter cold;
Attacking men and women who are old.
Smokeless fuel burns in the grate,
How, past years, we used to hate
The thickness of the smog and fog;
No more burning the 'death' log,
When bronchial chests became tight
The poor victims of a dense night.
After rain and tempestuous wear
Comes the clear, bitter cold air;
Sparkling frost stark and still,
Not a movement from the far hill.
Healthy glow shines from the race
As icy arrows bombard the face.
Coastal, inner urban or rural,
Displays its own particular laurel.
Sea gales, gigantic waves roll,
Town icicles droop from the wall;
The fields barren with hoar frost,

Homeless person's life could be lost.
That sudden blanketing of snow,
Ferocious winds frantically blow.
All the motor-ways blocked and bound,
There many a pile-up were found.
Gradually sorting out the mess
Was like playing a game of chess;
When the final check-mate came
Wintry-weather subsides, to calm, and tame.
Out of the blue, quiet and calm
Eureka! warming, healing balm;
Brief period of glowing sun
Ceased after a short run.
Nights tingled with frost,
Spasm of cold penetrated our bones,
Soon spears of ice stood out like cones.
Then that awakening blow -
Oh! earth carpeted with snow!
Early morning virgin-white is broken,
By first morn, risers awoken.
Trudging through the brittle park,
The broken clean expanse mark;
Bleary-eyed workers plod to work,
Giving it a patch-coat look.
Glistening whiteness becomes dulled
Many feet disturbed and muddled.
Murky, stark, barren sky
Brought chill, dark mire;
Like a black soul that is lost
To reign in hell at no cost.
Sun, then light will revive

And lost lands will arrive.
How beautiful creation from our Maker,
Illustrating the wonders, - no faker.
Can this blanket of snow so pure
Hide magnifitude, not lure.
How frost on the hedge-row,
Bodies shiver and feel low;
Venturing out from heated home
To walk, drive or roam.
Sitting on a bench in the cold air,
Lonely, isolated without a care;
Thinking thoughts that reminisce
With memories, that felt warm, like a kiss.
Will I slip into that ever slumber;
Then ever again to be one's lumber;
But again to wake to warmth,
Knowing that the cold backend has gone.

Country Aura

Travelling from town to country scene,
Likened from storm to calm,
My whole being is filled with ecstasy
With the fragrance of what I see:
The scented aromas fill the air
Expelling all unsweetened breath.
As I gaze over the quietened fields
Leaving behind bedlam and foul smells;
The stillness and beauty is rural itself.
I tread on the lush grass
And float across the meadows;
The wild flowers shoot up to me.
Fields newly ploughed or full of golden corn
Reflect their beauty for all to see;
Cows and sheep lazily graze with their newborn.
Hedges well slashed and ditches trim
Provide a uniform view;
Soon, leaving this aura of tranquillity,
I must go back to reality.

Seaside

Warm amorous sunshine,
Summer springing to life,
Branching rays emitting line,
Water sparkling like a sharp knife,
Beach stones on fire, cause fleeting feet,
Deck chairs parade in rows,
Sun beats-down on proms with heat,
Pier loungers sit in shaded bows.
Merry-go-round, sonorous music
Blares out deafening the deaf;
Thinking mind losing acoustic
Flimsy concentration, loose leaf.
New sounds rising to crescendo,
Bank holiday-makers, voices over-riding
Sea atmosphere showing waves of tremolo,
Searching quietness for hiding,
Disorientated, peace of mind low.
Move on, disgruntled man,
Find habitat of quiet and peace.

MISCELLANEOUS

Rural Landlubber to Naval Lubber

Young man labouring in the field: Springtime sowing
Golden seeds; Summer haymaking for fodder,harvesting
The golden corn to yield; pulling root crops amongst
The weeds.Dairy and fattening stock consume provender,
Toiling and sweating brow needs change He dreams of far-
Off venues,laying stretched-out in the barn: passing thoughts
Reinforce the range, leave these tranquil passive views
Looking for adventure greater than tarn.Strong rural frame
He has found from healthy air and wholesome forage.
Venture he may, tho' friends taunted, kitbag packed ere the
Sea draws him bound.

ii

Leaving all behind, full of courage set sail for a life
Undaunted. Joining the training fleet at Glendower hearty
                                        young
Man goes on parade: quickly promoted to deputy squad leader
Position quickly gained, quickly lost, all o'er. Hard life
For the green uninitiated, he now begins to study, foreign reader.
Medical terms, could not be more confusing, unhappy lad
Wrestling with theory. Subject to out-door life, manually
Free: now probationer toiling in wards, bemused. Absorb
Complexities slowly but fearfully, poor boy, gradually coming
To terms, does he? His shipmate seemed much less enthused,
Tended to 'encourage' a daunting influence. Jock was
                                          determined

To fail the test, "Ach! cissy work this" he said, he felt
He was abused, brooding each day and saying, for his defence,
"lat's be a stooker, at bast".

iii

Both tethered on the brink of defeat: drinking and chasing
To keep spirits up. Going ashore as oft', smoking tiddlers;
Then paired they up for a long-weekend feat, for a New Year
Celebration and good sup' from being Pompanians to
                                        Galasheilers.
A grand time he'll remember in Galasheils: food, toddies and
Beautiful girls galore. But, alas, back to the life at Haslar
Again to experience cerebrum reels and try slowly to fill
Voids as before, finding the white cells no easier. Nearing
The end of course to qualify: extent of knowledge to be tested;
Nervous and edgy, dull empty brain, sat rooted before the
Task, were they? The 'surge of their intelligence' arrested.
What matter, nothing to lose or gain.

iv

Reconciled to failure, affably, expectations limited
To transfer; results showed no doubt of pass for him,
But Jock failed miserably, alas, to meet again would
Never occur. Lo! no more probationer, no impasse.
Full blown 'tiffy' was he, displaying his red cross;
First draft chit to 'Kestrel', let loose among
Therapeutics, disinfectants, chirugical, sick bodies,
Doctor's whims, hypochondriacs to heal, treatments,
Laboratory staining and x-ray technology. Green, but
Fully pledged, stalked he assisting the M.O. who sussed

Out the greenness. Inexperience caused him to falter;
By mistakes gained knowledge aspired to be a most efficient
Sick bay tiffy, no less, skilled in x-ray, lab., minor surgical
Works and others. Now cast in a different mould unlike
The farm lad, before the change.

v

Interesting role to further all aims, mind becomes hardened,
Outlook cold, naval life has a wider range, besides medics
Learn new games. Besotted boy drawn to a life of guile,
Falling in for the liberty boat, with glee; diversified
Shipmates fall in for shore leave not to attend Winchester
Cathedral, 'but on the tile'. Arrive back on board at the lee,
Next morning a head full of grief. Two full years and half
Passed with joy, attending to officers and ratings galore.
Bandaging, suturing, x-raying and more: treating the clap
And isolating the spore. Gaining knowledge for his brain
To store, made the grade but what a bore.

vi

Uprooted from a life content, Chief informed him, 'draft
Chit, M'lad'; Doleful young man must stow his gear, locate
Kit bag and hammock, intent; 'new fields to plough', what
A pun b'gad. Cheerful goodbyes then out on the beer.
Love life was good, courting a gal; she from Whitley Bay
Held deep in his heart, Joan Frost pictured a love so
Strong. Every leave travelled he by rail, magnetic waves
Drawing a chart; bliss and happiness, Cupid couldn't fail.
Letter received formed the first seed, beloved joining the

WRNS. Pleading for her to remain a civvy, having no influence
On this stubborn deed: she joined at Reading, all women's
To train in a career as a Radio tiffy.

vii

First sight he had of this stubborn maid at Reading, dressed
In coarse navy-blue serge. Can this be the beginning of the
End of the romance? Now in Pompey on 'Duke of York',the
jade;
Home fleet draft waiting to sail and emerge.Received he a
Letter, not by chance, saying 'arriving Mercury' at Fareham
Next week; dated to meet at the club. Dressed in best 'tiddly'
Suit made of doeskin, donned he, steps out for shore leave,
Quite meek. High feelings suppressed by the unwanted cub,
Knowing her love is not a tight bond. Meeting and dating,
Sometimes viewing a film; walking, cuddling and kissing a
few.
Then sailing orders came to show the 'flag'; sailed out of the
Docks to an unknown realm; choppy Biscay seas, the hard
wind
Blew to buffet the carcase, pitch, tossing and rolling, thrown
Round like a rag. Two weeks before the mast showed exquisite
Dawn, destination Barbados after beautiful Azores.

viii

Unknown feelings swept through him like aethereal ecstasies
Never encountered or been born before; fierce tropical sun
Beating down full of glories, blue seas sparkling with high
Swell deep as dykes; white sand contrasting with azure

Calmness; crested waves beating upon the shore, all frothy.
Bobbing heads with black, tight curly hair; white teeth
Glistening and shooting and bombarding stars into space;
Caribbean black, rotund women gracefully perching bananas,
Precariously balanced, on crowns of hair, nonchalant and
Dilatory West Indian race. Light years away from his distant
Love, becomes acquainted with a Barbadian girl, innocent
Romance gave him a new sense of feat, playing truant, feeling
Guilty about the one above. Together dancing to calypso
Music, whirl; tropical rain cascading, perspiring with the heat.
Soon ship will up-anchor and leave behind romantic, alluring,
Aesthetic Island; inside deep calling to 'jump ship', paradise,
But sense of loyalty overcomes allurement; morose young man
Now leaving dreamland, sails to the island of Tobago bay.

ix

Forward to Tobago, Antigua and Jamaica, rising tides drift
                                                                                                    into
Slumbering swells. Straight, elegant coconut and palm
                                                                                                            trees;
Tranquil air in the garden of Eden with my Maker; calypso
                                                                                                      dancing
To spiritual ringing bells, swinging to and fro buzzing like
Wings of bees. Calling at the last island of the cruise,
RoyalMarines, smartly dressed, blue and red, dazzling white,
'Beat the retreat' to marching band in disciplined step.
Bermuda is lustrously like a jewel, washed clean with
Aseptic thoroughness. Travelling thro' heavy waters to
Norfolk muse; from dusky skins in the sun, to white, pallid
Skin so neat. Short aeon immersed in culture fuel; great

America with fabulous wealth greets 'cousins' as naval brothers
Leading them to paint the town 'red', local hospitality
Generous but sometimes left on their own, 'on the shelf'.
Inverted species not like any others tagging the 'limeys'
With shallow respectability. Fond farewells from 'showing
                                    the
Flag': homeward bound to England glee.

                           x

Ship's pilot safely manoeuvres, along the waterway, a grand
                                   old
Battleship into port with a 1100 complement, docks in
                                   Pompey
Harbour: battles she fought courageously at sea to fight
Unscathed victorious. Buffeting the seas again she went
Navigating western shores of Portugal and Gibralta. Latin
Races explosive but warm ensemble. Display of colours,
                                   radiating
like darting shoots of brilliant colourful lights; white
Top-domed dwellings stand out; walls hygienically shine and
Radiate; senoritas full of pulchritude, colourful,chaperoned,
Hiding behind variegated fans. Jack-tars 'savoir vivre' at
'Yoshiwara'; let him sow his 'wild oats', virginity lost with
                                   purity:
Boy into man, he sails the seven seas.The narrow streets of
Gib.with dancing senoritas,music from maracas shatter the air.
Gibraltar apes peer down squealing.

xi

Up anchor and away for sea trials, gliding through crested
                                             waves
Of azure, reaching knots to make the great bird shudder,
                                             deep
Down in the abyss of darkness, convulsing ocean trying to
                                             break
This 'great bird's' back; the gallant stokers overheat and
                                             profusely
Sweat causing saline dehydration and cramp. Sick bay
                                             tiffies
All alert to treat perspiring, red-hot bodies, to sooth;
                                             engulfed
In wet sheets to cool slowly reducing muscle
                                             convulsions.
Roll, pitch and toss as the great hulk gradually rides the
                                             gentle
Swells after heaving and tossing like an asthmatic attack.
Battened down, hatches and portal holes clamped shut,
                                             using
Ventilated air that turned oppressive; longing for sweet
                                             draughts
Of air to nourish lung sacs with oxygen.

xii

Ordeal completed, making for port, shore leave to console
                                             bored
Tars. Moving from bar to bar wandering, drinking,
                                             observing

Spanish dancing: petite feet stamp to music and glide with
Hands and maracal rhythm; soon to be forgotten, in the past,
              as
The Home-Fleet returns to homeport. This great hulk of a
               'bird'
Into dry-dock. Gallantly finished her 'chores' and now to rest:
              she
Is decommissioned and put to rest, to sleep she must, sealed
              with
A skin, mothballed, for retirement, a nostalgic emote. The farm
Lad, saturated with seagoing life, packs his kit, into 'Nelson' he
Goes waiting to be sent on a new commission. Where e'er
             will he go
Wonders he, then two weeks provides the answer,
            draft-chit to
Sunny Malta, what glee, attached to the hardy Royal Marines
            at Ghain Tuffieha.

        xiii

Perched at the north-end of the Island was his small neat
             camp,
A sea-going army of marines, khaki dressed: compared to a
             lonely
Naval tropical dress of white, one other with he, the M.O.
Down in the valley between his camp and the cliffs
            snuggled an
Army transit camp; commuting army and family groups
            to and fro'
To the shores of bonny England and sandy dunes of the
            Middle-East.

Jurisdiction had he for their medical needs as well as
                                      marines.
At the bottom of the cliff nestled a beautiful bay with
                                      lustrous
Sand and azure blue water lapping gently on the shore; the
Exuberant, blue sea of the Mediterranean. Tropical routine
order-of-the-day, afternoons free to swim and frolic at their
                                      special
Rock, habited by the chosen few, away from crowds in
                                      private recess
Daily to swim and dive into the deep blue waters and swim far
                                      out
To sea in the buoyant waters. Emerging gasping for air,but
                                      refreshed,
Now lying in the brilliant sun to dry off; then relaxing at the
Hotel at the top of the white cliff with local ambeet wine.

xiv

The thirsty,hot tongue now quenched from the heat back
                                      tothe
Camp for victuals and work. Each early morning muster of
                                      sick parade
Lined-up for M.O.'s inspection, coughs, colds, infected parts,
Discharging ears, epidermophytosis (fungal) for doctor to
                                      diagnose.
Treatments to alleviate pain, mixture and remedies
                                      dispensed to
Heal. Records and forms made up-to-date, ordering of
                                      drugs and

Dressing, instruments to clean and sterilize, the day hours
                                                                                       rushed
By; the evenings a trip to his local cinema, but alas called
                                                                                       out
Part-way through the film to clean and suture a wound or
                                                                               treat a fever.
Trips to Rabat and St. Julian's bay for local entertainment
And festival celebrations honouring the saints; the
                                                                                  snake-like
Procession of gaily, bright coloured dressed Maltese
                                                                               followers
Singing their processional hymns and displaying statues
                                                                               of the
Virgin Mary and epics of the Saint being honoured;
                                                                               Roman
Catholicism with its blind, mindless brethren trance-like
                                                                               into
The unknown realms of the spiritual world. Wine flowing
                                                                               freely,
Non-spiritual drunkenness; home-made food being gorged
                                                                               by over-
Obese patrons; monks making the opportunity while the
                                                                             sun shines.

XV

Continuing his afternoon leisure swims; competing against
                                                                               local
Football teams; then changes take place for his gain, an
Invitation to transfer to Bighi hospital at Valletta. Study he

Must for Leading-Hand and promotion rewarded; now to
adjust to
Ward-work and supervision of staff asserting authority and
Discipline, staff and patients benefited they. New-found friend
Boxer and athlete was he; healthy life outdoor training and
Participating in football, boxing, running and hockey, even
Weight-lifting, at the gym. Grafting and working to give body
Strength, abhorring the body-sapping routines, running
mile after
Mile on the lonely road psychologically detesting every
step he
Took; preparing a reluctant mind to generate enthusiasm to
Spur and propel him on for the next work-out and road
work. Oh!
For the comfort of his bed or a trip to Valletta and fill-up
With ice-cream sodas. Eating delicious cheese cakes, red hot
From the oven and drinking fresh ground coffee in a glass.
Listening to the music of great composers, symphonies,
operatic
Arias blaring out from radios, beautiful toned voices of
tenors,
Baritones, basses, sopranos, mezzo; Malta enthuses with such
Music. Operatic companies, at the theatre, billing famous
operas
That he and Bill delighted in.

xvi

But like all good things, time passes, back to the intermittent
Rain of England aboard a twin-engined plane. Return to Haslar
For the last lap, leading-hand fully established now is the

Time for gold to be displayed. Attending lectures to revise
Memory; studying Q.I.'s and A.I.'s as well, exams completed
Waits he for the result. Lo and behold, promotion came, badges
Of gold braid and golden buttons - Petty officer with one long
Service stripe feels like he's attained an Olympic gold medal,
So proud is he. Supervising his ward and staff affably,
Sparkling floors, beds lined-up, Doctor's rounds, then sister's
Rounds, bed tickets up-dated and treatments complete, patients
Tucked-up in their beds, longterm ones waiting for discharge.

xvii

The landlubber to naval lubber has now made the full circle
And returning to life as a civilian in a new adventure; career
Opportunities continuing in the same sphere, decides retail
Pharmacy as an attraction and joins an international
pharmaceutical
Company. At last the final demob day comes leaving behind
Fond memories: rushing waters have passed under the bridge
since
That first day 'before the mast'. Lo! a new life for the making
Unknown destinies lie ahead: vision obscured of what the
Future holds; one thing is certain: he'll miss his life at sea.

Surgery Muse

I sit in the surgery
Waiting for my friend
Listening to the chatter
Sending me round the bend.
My eyes look at each patient
Wondering how they feel:
They seem bored and latent
Do they want to reel?
The time drags slowly.
Receptionist chatters louder
I'm just amazed at them,
Because they are not quieter
At this special requiem.
Let their speech be lighter
So peace settles over this
Graceful waiting room.

Dunstan's Orderlies

Harken to the curses and swearing
Coming from the orderlies' room,
Ah! it's Harry talking to his mates.
They converse in another language
That rolls off their tongues with rage;
Expressive in its meaning,
That nobody can deny,
But sounds vindictive in its style,
With voices joining in at the same time,
Venting fury and humour in rhyme.
Now making crescendos
So all and sundry will know
That life in general is causing them to blow.
Sometimes they are renal
Many times aggrieved,
But best of all when lucky
Boast about the derby in Kentucky,
Finally ending up with a few pence in their pocket.

Overbearing

The woman young allures
All the time sending out impulses of love
Attracting the unguarded and unwary
Pulling them in, into her deadly backstream:
Knowing the foolishness of a male team.
Devious, scrupulous and enticing,
The slender, wriggling serpent
Overcomes the buck with venom
Never to let him go: until,
The last breath of life expulsed.
The poor writhing mammal, no escape,
She demands and dominates,
With high and mighty attitudes.
The consistant nag and leadership,
Formulating, directing to own design.
Allures pour forth and vocal soothing to
Prevent suspicion, allay fears
Of the mauled stag beaten,
Without reason or direction
Pauperised, penniless and lonely.

Dull Thoughts

Oh Mind! Oh Mind! of mine
It's dull and unresponsive;
The cobwebs veil the cells
And stilt the flow of words.
Brain patterns reflexively dull
Causing absent-mindedness acute.
This dismal unenlightened wave
Reduces thoughts that radiate:
Mind so retarded and blank,
Damn it! Where are the words?
Voids are forming in white matter,
To visualize has become blind:
Versatility ground to dust.
Poem, verse, sonnet and rhyme
Are jumbled up in and out of time.
Ah! tomorrow, Ah! tomorrow
Blow wind to turmoil;
Release me and clarify the picture,
Now I see quite clearly
Those beautiful thoughts to express.

Feelings run hot and cold

In the heart rivers run deep,
Life that is full of tributaries:
Feelings from the flow begin to creep,
The imprint of fallen obituaries.
Languid, dull and lifeless soul,
Emotions sweeping and tossing are cursed,
As they plunge into the deep hole:
No dam to stop the rising outburst.
Empty, deepening chasm in breast
Bewildered, unsure and now reeling
Saturated with bleakness to become depressed.
Hurt! hurt! cry out for healing.
Hiding behind false covered righteousness,
Blinding all with a sweet smile;
Erupting suddenly like a volcano, no less,
Exposing that bilious and sour bile,
Thrown in disarray from innocent sharing,
Spiritually disciplined not to offend;
Taut of mouth, no teeth baring,
Knowing tomorrow relationships will mend.
Guilt that is now in retribution,
Deep heart search for tributaries that do not bend.
Let it turn out to be an illusion.

Another Foolish Man

Quickly, quickly, security man,
Did you not hear me bleep?
I hailed you through the Tannoy,
"Smart up to the top floor
And see if the jilted man is asleep".
Rushing hither and dither, where is his abode?
Thank goodness here is the door,
Gingerly I knock in anticipation,
Come in, says a small voice, no elation.
Opening the door, there stretched out
Perceive a man full of anguish, out for the count.
Small bedtable lies an empty pill-box,
Panic sets in, don't do anything stupid,
I shout, she isn't worth it;
She's as cunning as a fox.
The poor foolish man left to rot.
His princess, richly endowed;
He , crushed under the malicious heel
And thrown out like useless garbage.
Haul him to the looney-bin;
Wife with no loyalty,
Is like receiving a punch on the chin.

Specky and Sister Fawn

Two sisters fight for rats;
They are fierce as wild cats;
Hissing and scratching is their game;
Be careful, long fangs make you lame.
Wild kittens come to our home;
No longer will they roam;
Fish and rice: morning and night,
No longer seek food and fight.
Sweet words impart and love,
Look bright eyed as I work above.
Speckly-brown coat, named Specky;
Light-brown fur is Fawn, and cheeky.
Fatten up and make content, peace
Giving our home a new lease;
Chasing and jumping from ambush;
Harken the noise of an onrush.
Fangs go deep and nip hard,
Specky lets out a squeal, now on guard.
The fight lasts until bored
Fawn departs outside like a lord.
Specky curls up to sleep
The pain made her weep:
But all forgotten 'til next affray
When Fawn again will strut away.
Small, loving Specky, purring aloud
Completely resigned and cowed.
Domesticated pet, homebird,
Fawn has still not heard,
Wanders away each day,

Meets her tom, to lay.
Lo behold! the big black tom
Specky runs like a flash hom.
Savage brute that he is
Turns her heart into fizz.
Jumping up to play with Den
Soft paw striking top of pen;
Now sitting and staring, ready to pounce
As she gives her last ounce.
Stretching out over my sheets of type,
Obstinate, adamant and full of gripe;
Refuses to budge, even one inch,
Now she's mastered me, it's a cinch.
Pleading and coaxing, to remove her stretched out form,
No quieter than an empty children's dorm.
The feline mind has me beat,
Alas, so'll resort to cheat.
Placidly stroking her furry tum
Treating me like her long lost chum;
Purring and stretching further still,
She silently slips over the table sill.
Broad smiles beam down from above
Saying, "I'm really sorry, love."
Oh! look, Specky is fatter
So young for kittens, does it matter?
Among the charcoal, her pride
Are two fine babies, which hide.
How sad we are, but they must go
And for a few days our hearts are low.
Specky running to her bed,
Where the babies had laid their heads.

Laying on my bed, stretched-out like silk
So I could stroke her full breasts of milk:
Gradually forgotten all in the past.
Then low and behold it isn't the last,
A bed in the wardrobe makes Fawn:
And has her kittens, but all are still-born.
Both with sympathy and compassion,
Inseparable sisters licking each with passion.
No more of this unhappiness, live
I inject them with a contraceptive.
Every three months I call them in
And insert the needle under the skin;
No more kittens, no more anguish
Now they have a life of languish.

Unearthly Hours

Oh, for the morn! Oh, for the morn!
What unearthly hour is this?
My head rests on its pillow
Next I jump out onto the dewy lawn;
Reaction to the semi-darkness is
Like a swirling mist on a field of fallow;
Then I become morbidly retarded
Alertness is diminished.
As I perform ablutions
And mechanically attire:
The mind is fuddled
Can there be a solution?
Shouldn't I once again retire,
Forcing my befuddled mind
To accept this heady situation.
Body and soul braves uncertain weather
As I tramp along the street,
Gloomy and silent as a ghost town;
Just the odd piece of traffic
Floundering to whom knows where.

Total Darkness

Hark the tap tap of the white stick.
Is the life of darkness sad?
Alas, I feel their loneliness -
Is it me that's blind and sick?
Who am I to be full of soundness?
To even think that they are bitter and glum;
Conceited man that I am.
See how light comes into darkness,
How they laugh and chatter
Making me a liar and shallow,
As I hear the darkness bellow,
'Mind the door and the shelf:
Don't bang yourself!'
A guffaw of smirk beats the air
Saying 'I'm not stupid, yer know.'
The guide dog pads its way along the pavement,
The escort leads at a slow rate,
White stick taps slowly along
But the misty eyes perceive every inch of the way.

Traffic Congestion

Bumper to bumper: tail to tail;
There's a taxi, give a hail;
But see, the traffic so dense
It's like a wall of metal fence.
The traffic lights are on stop
Vehicles come to a sudden chop:
Patiently waiting for the go
Hoping the stream will soon flow,
Nervous energy all pent-up
Waiting for the onslaught let-up.
Here it comes with that bright green
Swiftly moves the flow, all keen
Sounding horns, screeching tyres
Producing heat to burst into fires.
Morning, midday, evening rush
Causing frustration, and a brush
With the law, as tempers fray
Especially at the end of the day.
Obstacles cause the flow to halt
Bottle-necks put the stream in fault:
Drivers 'sit back' and accept their fate
Not caring about being late.
Oriental minds with poker face:
Day after day never lose face.
Weather so hot and humid outside
Using air-conditioning inside,
Slowly moving down the line
Experience congestion at nine.
Going to work in the queue

This is something that isn't new:
Two hours journey there, two hours back
The worn-out driver then hits the sack.

Apprentice Artist

Take a pencil by the hand,
Point to where thou wilt travel,
Sheet so empty like sea-sand,
Starting with a dot for the navel;
Unsure where to direct next encounter
Boldly strike a ragged line.
Now I again begin to flounder,
Creative art which is so fine
From left to right, no analysis:
Deeper thoughts, engrossed lobe,
Can it be a drawing basis?
Beauteous model wrapped in a robe;
Looking, looking intently at her,
Instinct guiding free hand
Eyes fixed on subject matter,
Detail after detail sets a band.
Time races by the hour:
Artist lost in obsession
Like climbing a high tower
Then falling into complete recession.
Shading parts to bring alive
Curves, lines and squiggles
Canvas buzzing like a busy hive
Painting complete all smiles.

Life in Arabia

Sand desert of Sahara, so hot:
Not the sand of the seashore, so cool.
Western eyes feel intense glare
Eyeballs burn into sockets
Fierce sand storms erupt
Cascading in all directions
Body pitted with particles so fine, stinging,
Hair now matted, turned yellow-brown.

Masticating sandy food, washed down
With sand precipitated drinks.
Oh! wholesome cuisine, where art thou?
Oh! Cool fountain drink, where art thou?

Observe North, East, South, West,
What do eyes perceive?
Glorious! no empty sand spaces, sand dunes
Reflecting intense heat.
Uncomfortable body, prickly and hot.
Natives in Arab dress, serene
Cool and placid, distinct aroma
Sickly, nauseating, strange.
When eating and drinking local style
Stomach fighting back nauseous eruptions
Arab finds normal and gastronomic.

Travels in the Imagination

Closing my eyes and thinking deep,
Suddenly thoughts begin to leap,
Imagining travelling to exotic isles
Cruising along for miles and miles.
Colours brightening each stop made,
Nothing to dull or even to fade.
Blue and red coaches dazzle my eye
Can stark imagination ever lie?
Taking me along at rapid pace,
The thrill of a lifetime, Is this the place?
Suddenly returning from a life long dream,
I'm moving along with a perfect theme.

Travels in the Imagination

Sweeping along on the crest of an incoming tide
Dreaming and loving this wonderful ride,
Flying serene on a cloud supreme
Holding tight to this exotic theme.
Beholding brilliant stars of light
Now travelling along on a full blown kite,
Tranquillity exceeds the joy I've found
Never to remain static and bound.
Freshness in glory, cruising along on stout wheels
Knowing the uplift and safety that feels,
Perfect in my inspiring ecstasy
Looking forward to my next fantasy.

Travels in the Imagination

Cosmic rays mingle with bright stars
Travelling to the moon in cars,
Computers directing all in space,
In this part of the world we have a different face.
Automatically shunting to Jupiter or Mars, with no fuss:
Nothing like the Brighton and Hove bus.
Zipping along at phenomenal speed,
Even time to dine and feed.
Atmospheric changes cause jet-lag head,
Now we can sleep it off in a celestial bed.
Moving gracefully between intercellar stars
This new era of travel will be taught in Mars;
Now peace of mind and no assault
Moving gracefully like an astronaut.

Ladyman

Harken to the lisp of the effeminate
High pitched with woman hate.
She struts around swaying her hips
And shows she can purse her lips;
When angry venom pours forth,
And the homo vents her wrath.
Beware the unwary caught
In case she entangles your thoughts:
First the hussy seems fussy
As lady-like flits around,
But soon stamps her feet
When realizes she is beat
Then Miss will sit and sulk
And pour forth venomous talk;
Swearing and vileness utters forth,
And the wrath of wickedness will stalk
Trying to entangle the naive to mate
Ending up in a masturbate.

LOVE POEMS

Our Parting Sorrows

How my heart yearns;
This is grief at its low.
But now I must learn
Is it time for me to go?
My sunshine is losing,
And my life is hollow.
Kobkul where can I go carousing?
I have no one to follow,
Life seems empty and lost;
All sparkle is now diminished,
Can it be such a great cost.
Is the will to love finished?
Please re-open my chasm:
My loneliness is but futile.
All of me is numb,
The world has done brutal,
Show beloved his peace.
That sweet spray I own
In the wilderness you have gone
Pray forever come to our home.

Heart's Desire

You are my heart's desire- I love you so,
When will you enter my life again?
The loneliness in my heart is thwart with desire for you.
Darling, not the licentious feeling;
Only the romantic companion aching to have you with me.
To walk together, bonded - talking over our
Interests in a rational way.
Eating our meals in harmony, being fully content -
Full bellies - reading our choice of literature.
Singing our love songs and hymns -
Quoting scripture, praising God.
Are we blind to each other?
Can we see what we are doing - persecuting
Each other because we have lost our ties!
The strong knot that secures you like a
Prisoner attached to your family and country -
My flimsy attachment is easily broken and
Remain alone and longing.
Why do I have a wife who will not hearken to her husband?
No authority or strength of character to give you confidence!
Must I wait till March before we look upon
Each other and glory in our reunion, -
Then torn asunder when you return to Krung Thep,
To wait one more year. What marriage prevails us
That two loyalties, nay three loyalties, unstabilise
The very foundations of a God-bonded relationship?
Many words express your love and loneliness, being
Separated, and held isolated from the other half of your life.
Does not your heart act, give you courage and strength of mind,

And say: "Darling, I'm coming to England to live with you."
No matter what happens from your decision.
I wait for that surprise.

I Miss My Husband

Another letter today I received.
My dear! How can you miss me so.
Full of endearments and sorrowful words;
You say your heart is bursting with grief,
And cried when my letter was late.
Oh! alas, your mother still reigns
As the hated Asian dynasty.
Can't you have one mind of your own,
And break the strings of steel?
Tyrants are more merciful,
Or even a Spanish bull.
Go to the blacksmith's and cut your bonds;
Then without any sound
Take to the air by wing.
As you fly look down and see the white cliffs:
You know Dover and England is home,
And safe from the idolatry ways of Buddhism.
Enter our home and tears subside,
Now you are free as the tide.
Bonded together never to part,
Oh! happy thou art.

My Wife and I

Just two bodies as one
As we ate and walked,
In bed we had no fun
But we feted and talked.
The days we rode in town
Many an argument burst out,
And angry exchanges in frown
But forgave and went about.
Our tiffs and spites were meek,
My dear, you never sulked
And always the first to speak:
Before night we talked.
God kept us reeling
Although He removed your desire,
But increased my feeling;
Lord, why did you bring us out of the mire?
At the resurrection our Father will enlighten us.

PERSONS

Strong, Courageous Woman

There was a girl named Alice
Who kept her house like a palace
Strength of character glowed from her
Every problem that came did not matter.
From young days smitten with ill health
She kept that smile without abundant wealth
Inwardly sick, outwardly full of courage
Alice fought with strength, no rage.
Losing her beloved killed by a Jap
He having fought secretly on an unknown map
Broken heart cried out, but not morale,
Readjusting from obituary and pernicious anaemia, this female
Fought back with tenacious stubbornness
To rise from the ashes, no less.
Absorbed her innards saturated with work
Day in, day out toiling never to shirk;
New love came her way named Shaun
Her eyes saw a tall, handsome Irish mourn.
Quiet, friendly and tame was he,
Directing his life like a worker bee
Joyful woman found the ideal man
Clucking and protecting him on her terrain
Outwardly glowing maternal damsel
Fresh with vigour and energy fanatical
Never a moment to rest from her task
To hide the dread disease like a mask.
Surface it will, and on that day fell ill
Large tumour of malignancy so evil;
Poor stricken body under the sharp scalpel

Incised a massive tumour called hell;
Weakened and demoralized from radium therapy
Accepted injections reducing her life dismally
Shaun was her strength and goal to hold
Fighting was her greatness asset to uphold,
Never to give in she fought with good faith
Raised herself from the shadow of death.
Only that man kept her on her feet
Waiting for the day when her Maker she will meet;
Fight she did for life was short
This great lady busied so it would not abort.
Two extra years of life she cherished
Pushing her energy to the full unpunished.
Bright, wonderful Alice dominant and sure
Lead their lives vibrant calling for more,
Moving here, moving there, directing both lives
Not giving in, to death which soon arrives
But in her heart she knew quite well
One day she would give in to the death bell,
And so it was one midday so peaceful deep
Laid on her bed and went to eternal sleep.

Adopted Mother

A Mother's eyes are smiling
Sincere, kindness, no lying
Watching and grieving as life goes by
Now it's your birthday, years fly.
Eight-three today, feeling quite young
Must find a song to be sung;
Adopted son stretch lungs and sing
Knowing it won't be like famous Bing,
Makes the air vibrant and lifelike
Over the hills through dales for a hike,
Only spiritually on banks of clouds
Enjoy just walking over mounds.
Lovely day for a great lady
Many more years of happiness, M'lady,
Jesus told us peace, love and care to all.

My Sick Little Boy

Hello, my sweet,
Whenever will we meet,
Granda so far away:
But I still think of you as I lay.
Though not so robust
But full in my thoughts I must.
You will grow like your brother
And I know there'll be no other,
For sickness you can endure.
I have a friend, the best
You could ever secure;
He is in me and I in Him
And I asked no rest.
Praying to the Perfect Man, Jesus,
To heal you and make the test.
Jesu loves you so very much
Give Him a chance to show
That He will stay with you,
No matter what you do.
Stop Granda's tears
As he prays to the great King.

Ludmilla

How I loved Ludmilla so very much
My heart felt her tender caress
She gave me interest unique
And opened my life fully.
Cupid and stars in head spun
Outwardly strong and bold,
Years between separated reality
Just looking down on my false youth.

Young, voluptuous beauty and fair
White as a lily and graceful hair.
Long legged and breasts so white
Smouldering fire within, flares up.

Dancing on air, floating along,
Startled by that sudden urge,
Beautiful Ludmilla can't be real
As she breaks the aura of tranquillity
Lisping and whispering words to distract
Drawing me into the web so tight
Obsessed with rapturous lust,
Fully amoured with melancholia.

Heartbreaks, apprehensions, suspicions,
Always torn by doubtful thoughts
Angry outbursts brought tears:
Leave me not, I plead,
All forgiven, tears subside
One day to leave for ever
The spark of youth that vitalized
The ageing fool.

Bright Eyed Boy

Loving boy so young and bright
Grandad's pride and joy,
Full of energy with abundant fun
Treating life just like a pun.
Healthy and strong: so sensitive,
Give Granda a kiss, my boy,
And share your love and joy with all.
Pushing toys from here to there
Becoming more ecstatic with glee;
Show them, son, that great big bear
The one that sleeps with thee.
Going to school, how time does fly,
It only seemed yesterday
I nursed you in my arms.
Maybe a score years I'll be using my stick
Chance it could be your arm:
One thing I know, if God permits,
You'll still be my bright-eyed boy.

The Scent of Ruskie

Love is so sweet in Ruskie
The drops of perfume so rare;
Scent smelling sour and fusty
Sweet damsels never seemed to care.

Reds, Reds, born into this,
Taken for granted,
Lack of water now unnoticed,
Odours filter from tissue bare
Fair-haired beauties want to share.

Winter, minus centigrade, freezing;
Summer, plus centigrade, sweltering:
Bathing in sumptuous waters, lament
Ruski says odours spell enchantment.

A Wee Scots Lassie

Here she is, oh bother me!
Her beauty lightens our very day;
She smiles with sweet pearls
And brightens my heart with an envious ray
Because I know she isn't of ordinary girls.
This damsel is the spice of life
And will make a young man a perfect wife.
She will know how to manage a household anew,
With her family just a few.
She isn't tall, she isn't short
But I would say she's the perfect sort.
A Scots girl born of a brae
Her voice detects the wonderful lilt,
Skin texture from the Lomond sky
A health and brightness we can't deny.
She will haunt us till the day we die
That bonny lassie from Scotland hi.

A Man at Work

What a man this is!
It isn't that he's in show biz
He stalks around like a clown
Grunting and looking with a frown.
Grudges and grievances abound
But what in his life has he found?
Complexion beams from inside
Looking to take somebody for a ride;
Yet he is the status of a peasant
Why does he always look for the present?
Maybe because he wants to be king
And life has not given him a fling:
When will he open his heart
And give us all a smile?
Then we can say, 'Good morning'
'How are you today?'

Her name is Sarah

Lightly she ascends the stairs
Quietly and serene with care
Slim with posture so graceful,
Even with fem or manly attire.
Smiling down like the heavens above
Behold! the beauty of a queen,
Dazzling complexion, radiant glow.
A mere maiden for the handsome interloper,
Shy, reserved, especially gifted
The friendliness sometimes evades her
Showing the mark of artistic temperament.
Geometric shapes and colourful shades
Expertly fill canvas with living colour,
Loving care guides her pale delicate hand,
Slowly the picture reveals the scene,
Ah! so real and lively.
Muted words from open full red lips
Make me feel despised and not wanted,
But so do others with some disdain.
That's Sarah for all to see
Young, tender, delicate, moody:
Embraced with her shadow
Alone she dances with vestige.
Breakout beautiful damsel
No introvert to restrict shining star,
Ripple the magic of your charm.
Watch! vibrations attract cupid
Smiling, holding deep sensations;
There is the far star, brilliant
Seeking this clear, clean starlet.

Lady of Remorse

There she is! Strutting down the road
With her dog on leash;
A smileless look comes over her:
Cold heart with a slow beat.
Bitter and sour most of her life,
When will she ever smile again?
High and mighty is the order of the day.
Though a lowly working life she leads:
White poodle and air of grace
Falseness is in her mouth and words
Voicing vindictiveness and curses.
Never a pleasant word to endure
Talking down like a mighty pillar,
A bitter, distraught, empty life,
Tender in years and become aggrieved
Gradually drawn, ebbed away.
Trying oblivion for her sorrows
Resorting to despair in sottishness,
When will she awaken and think?
Let brightness of character take over
Moulding and refining stature and mind;
Dazzling lights penetrate her conscience
Bringing out the true nature.
There she is! strutting down the road
Leading her dog with a leash,
Now bright and gay to see
No falseness or despair.
Just radiant light and confidence:
Light in her walk and alert of mind
How lovely this lady can be.

RELIGIOUS

Progressive Sanctification

Now I'm sanctified by God, The Almighty,
Does it make me high and mighty?
Do I flow light and free like silt
And brightest as the purest gilt?
Oh! blackened soul: now pure white
Depths of heart blessed and sanguine might;
Bathing in peace with solitude,
Stretched out and free of turmoil feud.
Alone, not lonely, basking in halcyon,
Oh! Love fill me Spirit overflowing on.
Strengthen the fortress round my being
Preventing black arrows piercing.
Deity is Judge and Punisher for all,
Fear the one who takes this Role;
Meek and placid awaiting his Will
Pedros the Rock is my fill,
Staunch, never diverting, any advent,
The grossness will not pierce or dent.
Conscience clear before the judges,
Though the accusations are smudges;
Weak as we are below, alas, shamelessly judging,
Omnipotence above compassionate, forgiving.
High and mighty alone are we
Our Maker so low and meek is He,
Transcend and reflect, Oh Beloved!
To make us humble, meek and loved.

Strengthened

Be strong in the strength of
Your Creator and Father;
Can He ever let you down?
Not one bit will He shy from
The decision He will give you;
Hark unto the voice of Son
And Saviour, as confident
Power surges into your
Spiritual charisma: Soul electrified.
Holy Spirit activated into
Powerful response, the peace
That passeth all understanding.
Now stand erect: see your
Way clear and full of light.
Jesus has you by the hand,
Leading and firmly directing
Body and mind, to the side of
Man, blessed with the marriage
Vows bestowed by him.
Loving silence of the air
Be still and motionless everywhere;
Don't murmur, be still!
Catch your breath, no
Muscle will ripple or move.
Tranquillity holds every
Movement spellbound. Alas,
The spell is broken, no longer
In the aura of stillness.

Sit, love, meditate,
Release all inhibitions;
Now empty of all iniquity,
Ready to receive the great
Power of our Almighty.
Live, live, live, Jesus is here.

Lord's Poem

I meet the great Lord
From morning to night,
Comforting me on my way.
All burdens become light,
Even when I can't endure.
He is my staunch friend
Right to the end,
Because Jesus is part of me.
Body filled with the Spirit
Is ready to fight the old life.
Demonic I may be
But the Spirit fights for me,
So I'm never defeated by the foe.
It could be that I fall
But God makes sure I recall
That punishment is in store for me.
Like a lamb I return to the fold.

Come to the Truth

Great Spirit-filled God,
Who ever dwells in me,
Jesus his name, my comforter.
Never forsakes or abandons,
Trouble and darkness He isolates,
Covered and anointed with his love
No one can harm or attack,
Protected in his shed blood:
The sinner wallows in the mire,
Fallen to the Devil's desires,
Makes the world an eternal liar.
With only one way out of sin,
Believe in Him and you'll win.
Lord and Master of all the saints,
Brother and Lord in bright array
Shining spectrum in the sky
Is righteous to arrive, now.
By obedience and Faith my Father staunch
Binds his children tight to love,
Sending them into eternal space.

Deborah

The Lord is your Shepherd
He leads you to fine places.
Jesus loves Deborah I know.
Pray to Him, have you heard?
Then you will see many smiling faces
With your heart full of glow.

Sarah

Sunshine radiates from your soul,
Loving eyes sparkle happiness,
Deep shadows overcome by light.
Jesus has told Sarah her goal,
The love that brings true gladness,
Brilliant moon shining down at night.

We remember

We remember,
We remember,
We remember,
Yet time goes by.
The nostalgia of the past
Leaves emptiness so deep,
Dreaming of far gone halcyon day.

We remember,
We remember,
We remember,
Every twinge of reality
Tearing into our insides:
Voids of despair, such loneliness.

We remember,
We remember,
We remember,
Old faces become a blur,
Yet vivid recollections
Turn on our sad refrain.

Woman with doubts

Fury of the wind she has
And stubborn as the sky,
Pursuing traits of paganism.
Utters her voice with atheism.
Dark blotches speckle on unfailing light
Like a vicious wolf's deep call;
Voice forming words ahead of thought.

Despair, despair! speaking tongue,
How dare you preach to me, born again,
In my way I believe, truly.
Healing powers in skeletal flesh,
Faith avails in perfect love;
Belial inside asserting force,
Changing her views, not clear.

Unsure grey cells dim wisdom,
Tongue-tied, mute and incomprehensible,
Expert voice unravels the mystery;
Now I sense the beginning of truth.

The Book of Life

Before time, we have been told,
Which was, is now, for evermore,
The Mighty One has entered in
Names, how formed, we know not,
Sit bold as life, brilliantly lit,
Apocalypse, Bibliography volume.

2

Strive we must for white apparel,
Clean soul, without sin,
Ten Commandments strictly adhere;
Love one another: No dissension,
Uphold father and mother: Good or evil,
Sexually disciplined: No wandering,
One God the Almighty: No small gods,
No murderous heart: Hatred none.
Light-fingeredness: Chop off your hand.
Sabbath is rest: Sunday is sleepy,
Use only your own: Take not from anybody,
Be truthful: Not even white lies,
Blaspheme not: Mouth words of respect.

3

Predained, elected for life eternal
Destined for immortality,
Not for death or destruction,
Pages and pages, names unknown.

How thick is the book of life?
(Should I say books?)
Even John of Patmos knew not.
Perfect man of God will reveal,
Shown as He comes through heavenly clouds,
Hordes to meet Him in the sky

4

Obituaries all forgotten, forlorn
Mankind in a dark abyss,
Antichrist perverting justice,
False prophets with a blank future,
The beast with the mark of death
Numbered on foreheads at tribulation,
Stubborn hearts, no Lamb's blood.
Not entered in the book of life.

5

144,000 chosen, tribes of Israel
Witnessing through perilous times.
Take heed! oh, you faithless ones:
The Lion, from tribe of Judah, Scion of David,
Pouring out His wrath at disobedience
Fresh prevails the weak and arrogant.
Scrolls read out, seals broken.
Not too late, turn back, take heed.

6

Satan, the dragon, pursues a
Pregnant woman, waiting
While she gives birth, ready
To devour the Child.
Male Child is raised-up to the throne of the Mighty;
Growing eagles wings she flies to safety,
Dragon spews water after her
Like a river to drown the woman;
Earth splits apart, water pours
Into its depths, she is saved.
Raging dragon rents his fury
On the rest of her offspring.

7

Persecuted, tormented and trodden into the earth,
The elected suffer fate untold.
History reveals the tragedy of the saint,
Canonized Saint, bear the scars of heat.
Romans threw them to the lions,
Then singing their hymns of praise met death.
Evil world, obstinate, will not repent;
Don't grumble, pagan, on the journey of no return.

8

God alone created life and death,
God alone created mankind,
God alone made nature from desolation,
God alone knows our hearts,
God alone decides our fate,
God alone will take our lives,
God alone wrote in the book of life.

9

Lord God of Heaven and Earth,
Messiah has now come for retribution;
Angels pouring bowls of wrath
Upon the unwary, causing pain,
Anguish, suffering beyond definition.
Plagues, diseases, earthquakes, famine.
People hiding in caves but unable to
Protect themselves from the harsh torments.
Sealed book of life, soon to be opened:
Did your heart change to believe?

10

Standing before our Maker, fearful and trembling,
Last days veil the darkness
Ultra dazzling, on fire, scorch and sear.
Blinded, stripped, humbled earthling,
No way to turn, cornered, the end.
Book of life is opened at judgement,

Heads bowed standing before God:
Lifetime of sin panoramaed in seconds.
Anger and gnashing of teeth for many
Unbelieving years; now, eternity of suffering.

Weak Christianity

Am I really on fire?
Or am I just a feeble liar?
Strengthening my mind with God
Did the One Supreme look down on me from Synod?
Iniquity easily comes to mind
Godliness seems far and aligned;
Spiritual adviser, clear my doubts
Fighting evil through many bouts.
Sunday after Sunday, clear message to hear:
But sometimes darkness makes me fear,
Saving Grace, Jesus, Comfort;
Prince of Darkness trying to abort.
Pray, pray fervently for support,
Angels of God protect and fought.
How can I doubt such Omnipotent,
Born again strong and potent,
Forever in the arms of Jesus,
Strong and upright, cause no fuss.
Oh! behold the day of redemption
Where there will be no exception,
Attitudes grieve and cause distress,
Flee from sin and unthoughtfulness.
Caught in devious and pagan taunt
Beware! darkness so pale and gaunt;
The way out! the only way,
Stand before Father in Prayer every day.

Spiritual Heartache

The suffering here is beyond my scope
But Jesus never abandons my hope;
Without his love and tranquil air
I would no longer care.
Inside the emptiness and void
Shine the light so I can avoid.
Empty shell, very desolate,
Holy Spirit fills to consolate.
Pray I may with fasting heart,
God, please remove this terrible hurt.
Day and night, night and day, close in prayer;
Father, no one but you, is my carer.
How church life shallow in quest,
But will not give up or give no rest.
Dark and dismal in my shell;
Praying for brightness to rise and swell.
Laying and thinking: deep in thought,
Will this longing to reach be naught;
Hallelujah! hallelujah! I shout so loud,
Then the curtain becomes a cloud.
Drifting through a malaise of guilt
Even the brightest flower would wilt.
Standing there, so bare and unprotected,
Touch my life, Lord, and make it effected.
Drop to my knees with anguish and despair;
Jesus! Jesus! do not let my heart tear.
Bathing myself in the Lamb's blood
Cleansed of sin from a water flood.

Close to God I pray in earnest,
Feathers warming me in the nest;
Hark to the sound of God's vibrations:
The Spirit within now full of elations.
He can no longer see me dull and lifeless,
Now will activate my calling and bless.
Far off, hot, humid destiny
Loving and caring even my enemy.
A Spirit filled life to fulfilment,
Away, away I cry with no guilt meant.